Something Fishy

Jacqueline Ross
Illustrated by Mark Wilson

KINGSCOURT / McGRAW-HILL

Something Fishy
Copyright © 2001 Rigby Heinemann

Rigby is part of Harcourt Education, a division of
Reed International Books Australia Pty Ltd ABN 70 001 002 357.

Text by Jacqueline Ross
Illustrations by Mark Wilson

Published in the United Kingdom by Kingscourt/McGraw-Hill, a division of the MH Companies. All rights reserved. No part of this publication may be reproduced or distributed in any form or by any means, or stored in a database or retrieval system, without the prior written consent of Kingscourt/McGraw-Hill, including, but not limited to, network or other electronic storage or transmission, or broadcast for distance learning. Originally published in Australia by Rigby Heinemann, a division of Reed International Books Australia Pty Ltd.

KINGSCOURT/McGRAW-HILL

Shoppenhangers Road, Maidenhead
Berkshire, SL6 2QL
Telephone: 01628 502730
Fax: 01628 635895

www.kingscourt.co.uk
E-mail: enquiries@kingscourt.co.uk

Printed in Australia by Advance Press

10 9 8 7 6 5 4 3 2 1

ISBN: 0-07-710320-3

Contents

Chapter 1 **Watson's Creek** 1

Chapter 2 **Creek Busters** 12

Chapter 3 **Stake-Out** 33

Chapter 4 **Mystery Solved** 48

CHAPTER ONE
Watson's Creek

JENNY AND KEVIN liked living really close to Watson's Creek. During the summer holidays, they spent lots of time at the creek, catching fish and wading through the clear, cool water on hot days.

Jenny's best friend, Jo, often joined them. Jo lived six blocks away from Jenny, but it only took a few minutes on her bike to get to the creek.

2 Something Fishy

Jenny and Kevin were next-door neighbours. Their homes backed onto the creek. Beyond the creek, partially hidden by trees, was a small industrial estate. The factories in the estate were also small. They didn't make a lot of noise or belch out black smoke like bigger factories did. It was easy to imagine that they weren't there at all.

Even though they were only half-an-hour from the city by car, Jenny and Kevin liked to pretend that they lived in the country. Watson's Creek felt like the country because the trees and bushes nearby attracted lots of birds, and wild flowers grew on the creek bank during spring.

Jenny, Jo and Kevin liked to compete with each other to see who could catch the most fish. Jenny was ahead.

The last time they competed with each other, she had caught twelve. Most of the fish were small, so they let them go after they had caught them. But it was fun trying to scoop them up in their fishing nets.

On the first day of the summer holidays, Jo rode her bike to Jenny's house, ready for a good day's fishing. Jo lived in an apartment and she loved

Jenny's big back yard and the creek that was so close. Jenny was still in her pyjamas when Jo arrived.

"Come on sleepyhead," said Jo. "Kevin's probably caught all the fish by now."

Jenny pulled on her jeans and a T-shirt and they followed the well-worn track at the back of Jenny's house that led down to the creek.

Kevin was already there. His fishing net was lying on the sand beside his shoes and socks. He was wading through the water, staring down into it.

"Don't tell me you've caught all the fish already," yelled Jenny, as she ran towards the water.

Kevin looked up and waved to them. "I wish I had," he called. "Hey, come and look at this."

Jenny and Jo both kicked off their sandals and walked into the creek. The sun had already taken the chill off the water. By the end of the day, it would be almost warm.

"Notice anything funny?" asked Kevin.

The girls gazed down into the water. "Where are the fish?" said Jo.

Normally a school of small fish would swim around their ankles as soon as they stepped in. Occasionally a bigger fish would pass, trying to keep well clear of them.

"You tell me," said Kevin. "I've been down here for quite a while and I haven't seen a single one." He waded out of the water. "There's something else. Come over here."

The girls followed him across the

sand to where several dead fish were lying, surrounded by buzzing flies.

"They must've been washed up at high tide," said Jenny.

"Yeah," said Kevin, "and there's a couple more around the next bend."

"That's really weird."

"Come on, you two," said Jo. "Five dead fish doesn't mean a lot. Maybe someone caught them and just left them there."

"But why aren't there any fish in the water?" said Kevin.

"Maybe it's the time of year when fish die off or something," said Jo.

"Well I think we should go further upstream and investigate," said Jenny.

Kevin and Jo followed Jenny as she walked along the sandy edges of the creek, looking for anything that might be suspicious. They had only been walking a few minutes when they found six more dead fish.

"Do you still think there's a simple explanation, Jo?" asked Jenny.

"It is sort of strange."

Kevin shook his head. "These fish are dying for a reason."

"And we're going to find out why," said Jenny, leading the other two back into the creek.

They waded through the water for another five minutes until they came to a sharp bend. Jenny was the first to turn the corner. She laughed as she felt the tickle of tiny fish against her ankles. "Hey you two, quick."

Jo and Kevin caught up, splashing the water as they ran against the gentle current.

"The fish are back," said Jo. "There's loads of them here."

"Let's get our nets," said Kevin.

Jenny put her hands on her hips. "Forget the nets. We've got a mystery to solve."

"But how?" said Kevin.

"We just need to think about it, that's all." Jenny paced up and down the beach, chewing on her fingernails.

Jo and Kevin sat down on the warm sand to do their thinking.

After a few minutes, Jo spoke up.

"If the fish up here are okay but the fish down by your place are all dead, then the problem's got to be downstream."

Kevin nodded. "Yeah, but what's different down there?"

Jenny picked up a pebble and sent it spinning into the creek. "I've got it all worked out," she said.

CHAPTER TWO
Creek Busters

AFTER SHE'D WATCHED the pebble skim across the water, Jenny flopped down onto the sand and stretched her arms above her head.

"I am just an absolute genius," she said.

Kevin and Jo looked at each other and smiled.

"Okay, Jen. What's your brilliant idea?" said Kevin.

Creek Busters 13

Jenny sat up. "What's downstream but not upstream?"

Kevin shrugged.

"I know," said Jo. "The industrial estate."

"Exactly."

"So what?" said Kevin.

"So, the factories are poisoning the fish. Someone's dumping stuff into the creek and it's killing them."

Kevin looked confused. "What kind of stuff?"

"Things that are poisonous to fish, like chemicals or oil."

"But why dump it in the creek?" said Jo.

"Because it costs lots of money to get rid of it," said Jenny. "My uncle's got a take-away food shop and he has to pay someone to come and get all the used oil. It has to be thrown out in a special way so that it doesn't hurt the environment."

"Really?" said Jo. "I'll bet it's the chip factory then. Think how much oil they'd have to get rid of."

"Let's sit down and make a list of all the possibilities. Then we can go looking for clues," said Jenny.

The four factories that backed onto the creek were the most likely culprits. Besides the chip factory, there was a workshop where cars were repaired and serviced, and an oil paint factory. Either place could be dumping oil. The fourth factory made rubber hosing.

"I think we should just go to the police," said Kevin, "and get them to sort it out."

Jenny and Jo agreed, although Jenny secretly hoped she could solve the mystery herself.

They wrapped a dead fish in newspaper and took a bus to the local police station. The officer at the front desk smiled when they walked in.

"Hello, kids," she said. "Enjoying your holiday?"

"Yes thanks," said Jenny, "but we've got a problem."

"What's that then?"

Kevin put the parcel on the desk and unwrapped it, revealing the dead fish. It was a hot day and the fish had begun to smell a bit. The police officer took a step backwards.

"The fish are all dying down at Watson's Creek," said Jenny. "We think something fishy's going on." She hadn't meant to say that. It had just slipped out.

The police officer grinned. "All fish have to die sometime," she said. "Although, judging by the smell, I'd say this one has been gone for quite some time."

"You don't understand," said Kevin. "There used to be loads of fish in the creek down near my place but now they're all gone."

"Look kids, I'm afraid we've got better things to do than worry about a few dead fish."

"But it's more than a few," said Jenny.

"I understand that, but it's hardly a serious crime, is it?"

"We think they might be getting poisoned by one of the factories."

"You've all been watching too much TV. Why don't you go to the swimming pool or something? Take your mind off it."

Jenny started to protest. "But we—"

The police officer held up her

hand. "Sorry, kids, no time to talk. I've got a pile of paperwork to do. Have a nice swim."

Jenny sighed and the three of them turned and headed towards the door.

"Don't forget this," said the police officer, pointing at the dead fish.

The sun beat down as Jenny, Jo and Kevin walked to the bus stop.

"I'm going to melt," said Jo.

Kevin wiped his forehead on the sleeve of his T-shirt. "Fry, more like it. Sizzle up till there's nothing left of us."

"Will you two stop complaining?" said Jenny. "This has worked out great. Now we get to solve our very own mystery."

"You *have* been watching too much TV," said Kevin.

Jo laughed. "It's a good idea though. Hey, we'll be like private detectives."

"Yeah. I'll be Detective Kevin."

"And I'm Inspector Jo."

"We need a proper name," said Jenny. "A secret name that no-one knows except us. What about the Secret Three?"

Jo smiled. "No offence, Jen, but that's not very original."

"I suppose not."

"What about something with the word 'fish' in it?" said Kevin.

"Maybe," said Jenny, although she didn't think the word "fish" made them sound like a proper team of detectives. "Hey, what about Creek Busters?"

"I like it," said Jo.

Kevin smiled. "Me too."

"Okay then, Creek Busters, let's start looking for clues," said Jenny.

"I think we should start with the chip factory," said Jo. "We'll go there and ask for a guided tour."

"I'd like to tour a chip factory," said Kevin, who was always hungry.

Jenny nodded her agreement. "Right. What are we waiting for?"

"The bus," said Jo, laughing.

22 Something Fishy

The chip factory was called Crispy Bites. They made chips in lots of yummy flavours. Jenny and Kevin liked chicken-flavoured chips the best but Jo's favourite was sour cream and onion. Before they'd even begun to look around the factory, the owner, Ms Reed, had given them some free samples to take home.

Ms Reed was very friendly. She was only too happy to let them look around the factory and show them how chips were made. The Creek Busters got to taste lots of chips during their tour, but they tried not to let the chips distract them from looking for clues.

At the end, Jenny was feeling a bit nervous because she had to ask Ms Reed a very important question.

They'd tossed a coin before they went in to see who would ask her. (It was only between Jenny and Kevin because Jo sometimes got a bit tongue-tied when she was nervous.) Jenny had lost the toss. She didn't want Jo and Kevin to know she was nervous, so when she spoke her voice was really loud.

"How do you get rid of all your old oil?" she asked so loudly that Ms Reed nearly jumped out of her skin.

"Oh...um, that all gets recycled. A special collection truck comes and siphons it off for me every Friday."

"That's what we thought you'd do," said Kevin who was hoping for more free samples.

After they'd finished the tour, they sat down by the creek and talked about the clues they'd each found. There wasn't much to say. No-one had found any clues at all.

"But she sounded really suspicious when I asked her about the oil," said Jenny. "It took her ages to reply."

"You yelled at her," said Kevin.

Jenny went red. "Anyway," she said, "all we have to do is look out for the oil collecting truck on Friday. Then we'll know she's innocent."

Next, they visited Mr Potter who owned Potter's Oil Paints. He wasn't nearly as friendly as Ms Reed was.

26 Something Fishy

He didn't offer them any free samples.

"There's not much to see," he said as they followed him into the factory. "Paint gets mixed up in the big vats then piped along to the conveyor belt to go into cans."

The paint factory smelled really bad. Kevin was feeling a bit sick because of all the chips he had eaten. Fortunately, the tour was very short. "Can't waste any more time with you kids," said Mr Potter before they'd had a chance to look for any clues. "Run along now."

The Creek Busters thought that his behaviour was suspicious. They hadn't had a chance to ask him how he got rid of any excess paint, although they all doubted that he would have told them. All they could do for the moment was carry on with their search and visit the next most likely suspect—the car service centre, Ted's Motors.

Ted and his mechanics all seemed really busy. The workshop was crammed full of cars. There were lots of large drums all over the place. Each one looked like it could contain oil.

Ted was very friendly. "Hi, kids," he said when he saw them. "I'm Ted, the boss. I'd shake your hands, but look." He grinned and held out his hands. They were black with grease. "You kids like cars?"

"I do," said Jo. Her mother had just bought a brand new red car. Jo loved going for rides in it.

Kevin liked motorbikes better, but he nodded anyway. Jenny was only interested in finding clues. "We'd really like to have a look around," she said.

"No problem." Ted led them towards a silver car that had been jacked up into the air. Two mechanics were working underneath it.

"We do all sorts of work here. Everything from a major engine rebuild to a simple grease and oil change. Depends what the car needs."

"Oil change?" said Jenny.

"Yeah. All the time."

"What do you do with the old oil?"

Ted stared at Jenny. "Now, that's a funny question. I thought you'd all want to ask questions about this beauty here."

30 Something Fishy

Ted patted the silver Chevrolet. "It's a 1972 model, fully restored and runs like a dream. First we rebuilt the engine then we worked on the body for weeks..."

The Creek Busters tried to listen to what he was saying, but their eyes were flitting from side to side as they looked for anything suspicious.

After they'd finally left the workshop, Jo suggested that they go and look for clues around the back.

"Did you see all those drums of oil?" she said. "And it was strange the way he changed the subject when we asked him about it."

"I'll say," said Jenny. "I think he might be the one."

The Creek Busters walked right around to the back of the workshop.

There were a few car wrecks parked out the back but nothing that really seemed suspicious until—

"Hey, come here," called Kevin. "You won't believe what I've just found."

CHAPTER THREE
Stake-Out

Kevin was standing at the start of a well-worn track that led down to the creek. The track started outside the back entrance to the car workshop, beside a big set of double doors.

"They could roll drums out of here really easily," said Kevin.

Jo nodded. "And look how wide they've made the track. You wouldn't need it that big just to walk down."

"Not so fast," said Jenny. "It might not mean anything."

Jo had to agree. "Jen's right. It's not real evidence. Why don't we camp out overnight and take turns at watching the place?"

"Good idea," said Jenny. "A stake-out."

Jenny could just see the workshop through the trees from the very back of her garden. It was the perfect spot to watch without being seen.

The night of the stake-out was hot. Jenny's parents didn't mind the three of them camping out in Kevin's big blue tent that they pitched at the bottom of the garden. Jenny's dad made them his famous pepperoni pizza and they ate it in the tent. Then Kevin offered around his chocolate collection, which was what he spent most of his pocket money on.

They all took turns at watching the workshop. One person was on duty for two hours while the other two slept. At first it was really exciting, but after about six hours and no movement at the workshop, it began to get pretty boring.

Jo got especially grumpy when she was tired, so Kevin and Jenny let her go on duty for one hour at a time instead of two. They felt annoyed when it was Jo who saw the lights go on at the workshop at 4.00 a.m. during her shift, but they tried not to let it spoil their excitement.

After climbing over Jenny's back fence, they waded through the creek in their running shoes. The trees and bushes were a bit spooky at night, and the creek made a rushing noise that none of them had noticed before. Jo wished that she hadn't just read a scary book about a creature that lived in a creek and attacked children.

They walked through the bushes to the back of the factory, their wet shoes making squelching noises with each step.

The only way to see into the factory was through a very high, small window. Jenny stacked up some old wooden boxes she found nearby so that they could climb up and peep through. Then she scaled the boxes and looked into the window. She could see the mechanic rolling a large drum across the workshop—a drum that was probably filled with oil.

Jo and Kevin couldn't wait to find out what was going on. There was just enough room for them to climb onto the boxes, too, if they hung onto Jenny and climbed up carefully.

"Hey," whispered Jenny, "it's not safe for all of us. You'll have to—"

Suddenly, the boxes beneath them collapsed and all three children landed on the ground.

"Ow, my backside," moaned Jo.

Jenny gave Kevin a shove. "Get off my arm."

"Well, I can't if you're on my legs, can I?"

No-one was really hurt. But they all knew that they'd made an awful lot of noise.

"We'd better run for it," said Jenny.

But it was too late. The dark shape of a man loomed up in front of them.

"What are you kids doing out here?" said a deep voice.

"Um...nothing," said Jo.

Kevin stood up and brushed himself off. "Um...just going for a walk," he said. Once Kevin had had a good look at the mechanic, he didn't really look scary at all.

"A walk? At this hour?"

Jenny and Jo stood up, too.

The mechanic shook his head. "You sure gave me a fright. I thought someone was trying to break in."

No-one knew what to say.

"Anyway, I reckon I know what you were up to," he said with a smile.

Jenny felt her heart lurch. "You do?"

"Yep. It's the best time for fishing around here, isn't it."

All three of them just smiled.

"You lot have found my secret track. It leads to the best spot. I used to fish a bit in the mornings. Been too busy lately though."

"We used to fish, too," said Kevin, "except now there's no—"

Jenny stood on his toe. Hard.

"So," said Jo, "if you're not going fishing, what brings you to work so early?"

"I'm restoring an old car for my parents. It's the car they used when they got married. It's their thirtieth wedding anniversary in a few weeks and I want to surprise them."

The Creek Busters looked at each other, meaningfully. Ted's Motors was no longer a suspect.

It was hard to know what to do next. On Friday, they planned to watch out for the oil disposal van that took away the waste oil from the chip factory. If it arrived, and they all thought it would, then that would definitely rule Ms Reed out as the criminal.

They decided to go back and investigate the paint factory more thoroughly, even though no-one really knew where to start.

"Hang on, I've just had a brilliant idea," said Kevin. "Give me your drink bottle, Jo."

Jo passed him her clear plastic bottle. Kevin raced down to the creek and collected a sample of water.

"Kevin, that's disgusting. There could be anything in that water."

Kevin didn't hear. He was holding the water sample up to the light.

"What are you doing?" said Jenny. "Apart from wrecking Jo's bottle."

"I remembered something from science. Come and look at this."

The girls went down to Kevin and stared at the water in the bottle. It looked a bit murky, but there was nothing unusual about it.

"So?" said Jenny.

Jo smiled. "It's not separating."

"Exactly," said Kevin.

Jenny looked confused.

"You see," said Kevin, "if there was oil in the water, it would separate out and float on top."

Jenny nodded. "So whatever is polluting the water, it isn't oily. That counts out the chips and the paint."

"So the only other factory in the right area is the rubber hose place," said Jo. "But what could they be doing?"

Jenny shrugged. "I don't know, but I think we'd better find out."

Mr Hackett, owner of Rubber Hoses Unlimited, was very happy to show them around his factory. He was so helpful that the tour took ages. By the end of it, the Creek Busters hoped they would never hear anything about rubber hosing ever again.

At the back of the factory was a large stainless steel door with a padlock on it.

"Can we have a look out there?" said Jenny, when the tour was over.

"No," said Mr Hackett quickly. "It's private."

The Creek Busters looked at each other. It was enough to make him a suspect.

After they'd left the factory, they went down to the bit of creek that ran right behind it.

"There must be something down here that'll give us a clue," said Jo.

Kevin and Jenny were looking through the bushes, carefully working their way around each one so they wouldn't miss anything.

Kevin didn't sound very hopeful. "Can't see anything here."

"Hang on," said Jo, "look at these funny lines in the sand."

Jenny and Kevin walked down to the sand where Jo was standing. There were odd wiggly lines in the sand.

Jenny studied them carefully. "Looks like something's been dragged across the sand."

"You're right," said Kevin. "Something sort of snakey."

Jo smiled. "Yeah, like a hose."

CHAPTER FOUR
Mystery Solved

THE CREEK BUSTERS gave each other the thumbs-up sign. They were really getting somewhere now.

"I propose we have another stake-out—tonight," said Jenny.

Kevin and Jo agreed straight away.

Just like the first stake-out, it was ages before anything happened. Then around 3.00 a.m., during Jenny's shift, a large tanker pulled up outside the rubber hose factory. Written in big red letters on the side was, "Danger Toxic Waste".

Jenny woke the others up. Even Jo jumped out of her sleeping bag as fast as she could when she heard the news.

The Creek Busters found a secluded spot in the bushes across the other side of the creek. It was as near to the tanker as they could get without being seen.

As they watched, Mr Hackett came out from the back of the factory through the big steel doors. He was carrying a thick rubber hose which he attached to the tanker.

The Creek Busters were so excited, it was hard not to talk to each other. But their position was very close to the action and they couldn't take the risk of being heard. They didn't want anything to go wrong this time.

Jenny wished that she could take a photo. She had slung her camera around her neck before they left the tent, but it would be too risky to use the flash.

Before long, they saw the rubber hose snaking across the sand and clear liquid flowing into the water. The Creek Busters looked at each other. They'd cracked the case. It was very exciting. They wanted to clap and shout and jump up and down. But they had to be quiet. So they just smiled at each other instead.

Whatever was being pumped into the creek was frothy-looking and smelled really awful. Kevin had to hold his nose.

After about ten minutes, which felt like ten hours to the Creek Busters who couldn't talk or move around, Mr Hackett went back to the tanker.

He disconnected the hose. The truck driver soon joined him and they shook hands.

"Right then, see you Thursday," said Mr Hackett.

Jo was so excited she whispered, "We've got him," in Jenny's ear.

Jenny was too busy writing down the registration number of the tanker to reply.

When they got back to their tent and the lights at the factory had all gone out, the Creek Busters jumped up and down on their sleeping bags. They chanted, "We did it, we did it, we did it, go-o-o-o Creek Busters."

To celebrate, Kevin gave each of the girls a whole chocolate bar from his collection.

It was a hot night and the chocolate melted while they ate it. When they had finished, they licked the foil wrappers to get the last little bit of the yummy treat. Then they talked about what they should do next.

Jo was concerned about going back to the police. "How do we know they'll believe us this time?"

"I knew I should've taken my tape recorder," said Kevin.

"We were too far away; it wouldn't have picked up anything," said Jenny. "I'm sure we can get the police to check out the registration of the tanker. Plus we've got a definite date for the next crime. They're bound to listen to us now."

Jo and Kevin looked at each other. They weren't so sure.

When the Creek Busters arrived at the police station, they were really pleased to see that there was a different police officer standing behind the desk. They smiled at each other when they read her name badge. It said, "Constable Watson".

Jo looked across at Kevin. "Maybe that will bring us good luck," she whispered.

The police officer listened to Jenny while she told their story. She didn't interrupt or give them a funny smile once. In fact, she was so interested she said that she would talk to the other officers about it at once and see what they could do. The Creek Busters left the police station feeling hopeful.

The next day, Jenny got a phone call from Constable Watson. She'd promised them that she would call and Jenny had been sitting by the phone all day. She had not let her little brother use it once, no matter how much he annoyed her.

"Jenny," said Constable Watson, "you three kids have done really well. We've had the creek water tested and chemicals have been found in the samples. I'd say Mr Hackett has been making a fortune getting rid of the toxic waste from chemical factories."

Constable Watson said the police would watch the factory on Thursday night and see if they could catch Mr Hackett and the tanker driver in the act. Jenny was so pleased she was bouncing up and down on her toes as she listened, but then came the best part of all—

"If your parents agree, I don't see any reason why you three couldn't watch the whole operation from across the creek. We'd station one of our junior officers with you, of course. But we don't think that Mr Hackett is dangerous and he certainly won't be expecting us."

"Could we? Could we really?" asked Jenny, her stomach churning with excitement. This was more than they had expected.

When their parents found out what the Creek Busters had discovered, they were so proud and excited that they came to watch as well.

It was 4.30 in the morning before the tanker finally arrived. Jenny felt scared that it wasn't going to show up, but when it finally did things went really well. The police caught Mr Hackett red-handed.

Mystery Solved 59

Everyone watched him and the tanker driver being handcuffed and put into the police van.

Everything worked out better than the Creek Busters could ever have imagined.

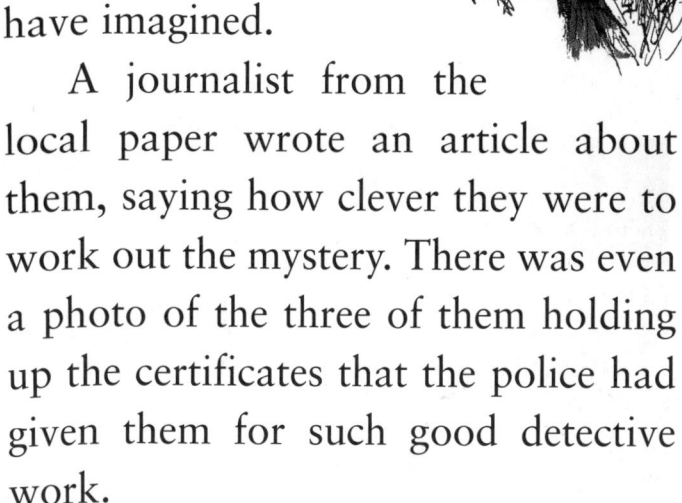

A journalist from the local paper wrote an article about them, saying how clever they were to work out the mystery. There was even a photo of the three of them holding up the certificates that the police had given them for such good detective work.

The best part of all was when the creek got cleaned up.

In no time, it was teeming with healthy fish again. Jenny, Jo and Kevin all agreed that nothing in the world could be better than that.